How to Make a Humane Animal Trap

Suitable for Rats, Cats and Small Animals

Includes Drawings and Construction Plans

by

Andrew Walters

andrew.walters.design@gmail.com

http://andrewwaltersdesign.com/

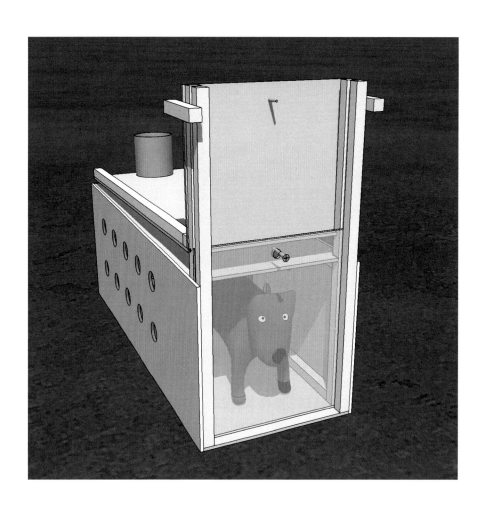

Contents

Introduction - The Prototype

We had a rat in our pantry!

Couldn't catch her, or persuade her to run away (yes - it could have been 'him'), so we had to trap her.

We live miles away from anywhere that sells humane traps, so I decided to make one.

My first attempts were based around a design that required the weight of the rat to trip a mechanism that would pull a pin, or release a spring - letting the trap door fall to the closed position.

Didn't work! I know because on the morning after each attempt, the trap door was open, yet there was no food inside!

I realised that the problem was that there was too much friction in the mechanism to enable it to work by depending on the weight of a tiny rat to operate it.

A radical rethink and I came up with this design, which does not depend at all on the weight of the animal to operate it. Instead, the mechanism relies on a prop to hold the pin in place which in turn, holds the trap door open. This prop rests on a small tray of food. For our rat, we placed some dry cat crunchies in a cardboard tube (yes - a toilet roll tube) which was cut to be about 30mm long. The prop rested on the food. The mechanism operated on the principle that, the rat would eat the food (because that's why he was there), as the food was eaten, the prop would drop, releasing the holding pin, allowing the trap door to close.

It worked!

Here he is behind the perspex screen. At the back of the trap you can see the prop, resting on the (part depleted) tube of cat crunchies.

The picture on the right shows the pivot mechanism, resting on the prop. The extra weights are added to overcome any frictional losses, thereby ensuring that, as the prop drops, the pivot turns, and the trap door closes.

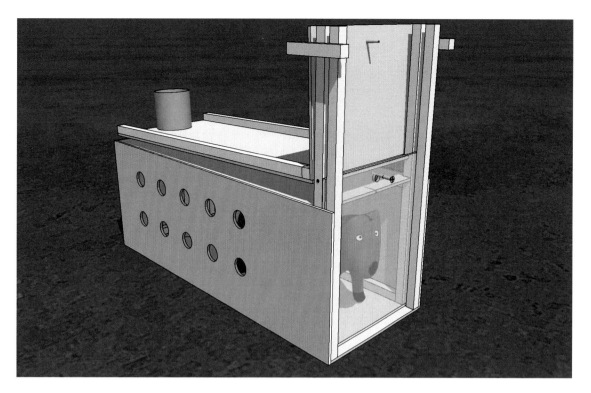

The Design

This design is a development and refinement of the prototype design and has been increased in scale, so that it is suitable for catching animals as large as cats.

For this design, economy of material use has also been considered. One trap can be made from one 8' x 2' (2440mm x 610mm) sheet of 1/4" (6mm) plywood with very little wastage.

In terms of cost, at November 2013 prices, the plywood and timber battens could be bought for less than $15 from Home Depot in the US, and less than £15 from Wickes in the UK.

The size can be adjusted to suit your own requirements - smaller for mice, larger for dogs.

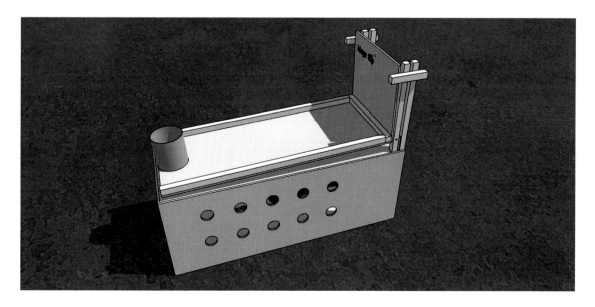

Operation

The following illustrations show how the trap operates......

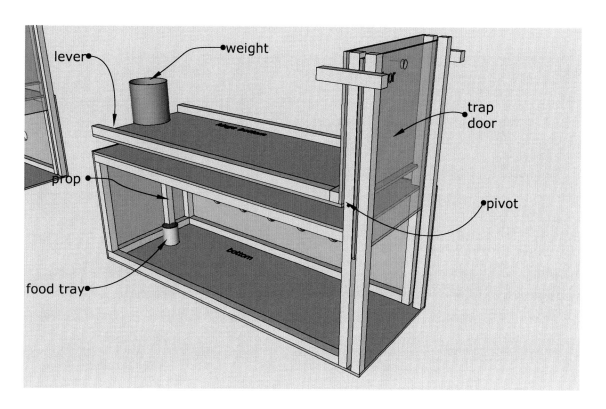

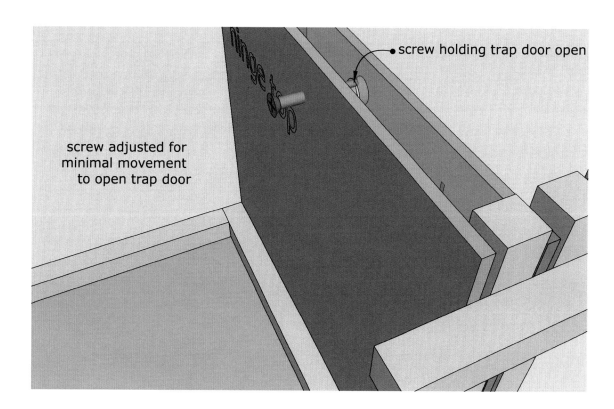

prop held up by food in tray

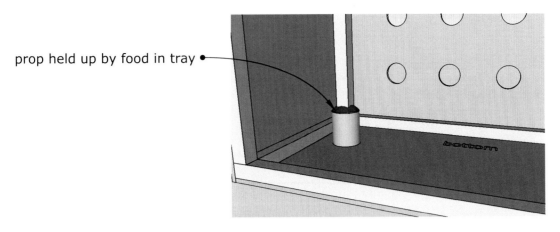

as the food is eaten,
the prop is lowered

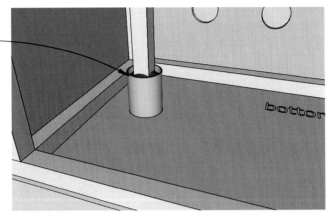

the lowering of the prop causes
the lever to move, releasing the
screw from the trap door

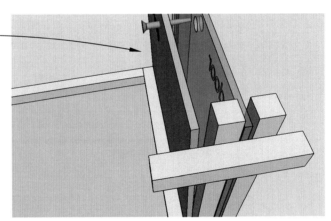

and, as the screw is released, the
trap door falls and closes the trap

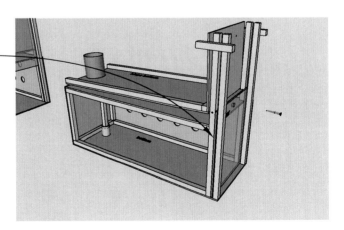

Operational Notes

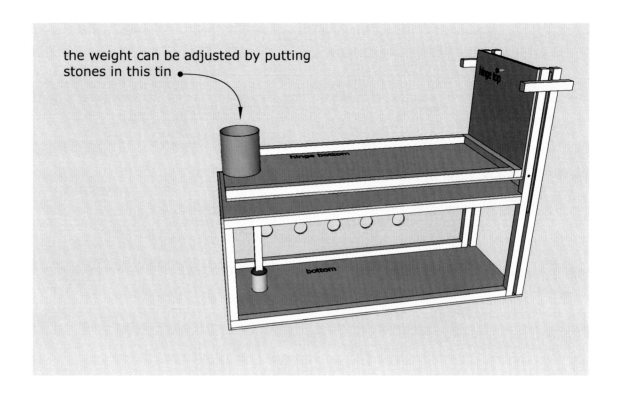

the weight can be adjusted by putting stones in this tin

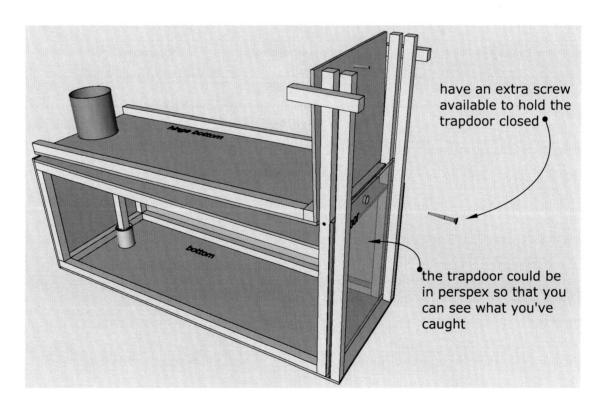

have an extra screw available to hold the trapdoor closed

the trapdoor could be in perspex so that you can see what you've caught

Materials

This trap has been designed to be made from 1/4" (6mm) thick plywood, primarily because it is cheap, light and readily available.

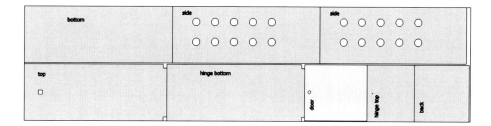

Plywood:

One sheet;
8' long x 2' wide (1220mm x 2440mm).

Softwood Battens:

3/4" (19mm) square;
About 24' (7.2m).

And:

1" (25mm) screws;
two longer screws about 2" (50mm) long for the trap door;
an empty food tin to contain the counterweights;
a cardboard food tube (empty toilet roll) - narrow and tall rather than short and wide;
some pebbles as counterweights;
some food - cat crunchies are good.

Tools

A battery drill / screwdriver for drilling the holes and putting in the screws.

Drill bits, screwdriver bits, a holesaw approximately 1 1/2" (38mm) diameter.

A handsaw for cutting the wood. I'd recommend a Japanese pull saw.

A circular saw for cutting the plywood - alternatively, buy the plywood from a place that will cut it for you. It will save a lot of time.

The Panels

The drawing below shows the cutting layout and dimensions for one trap.

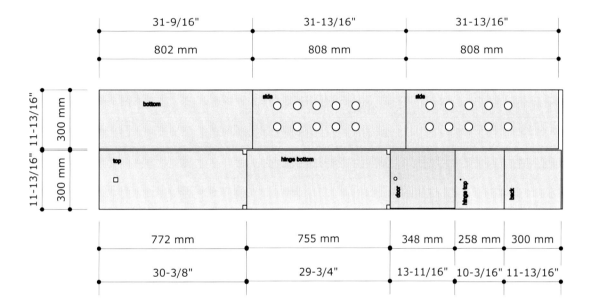

The Panels

The drawings below show the cutting dimensions for the trap panels.

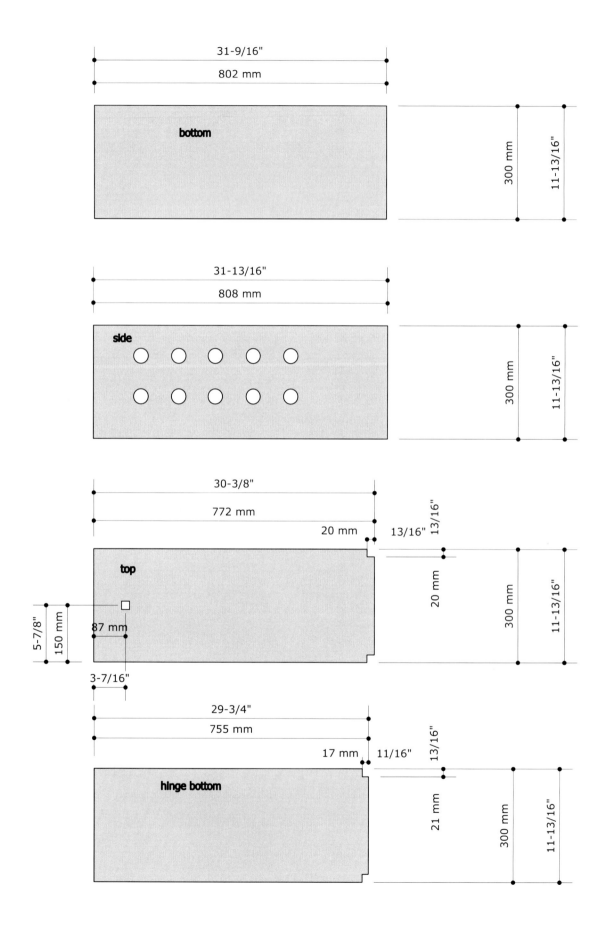

The Panels

The drawings below show the cutting dimensions for the trap panels.

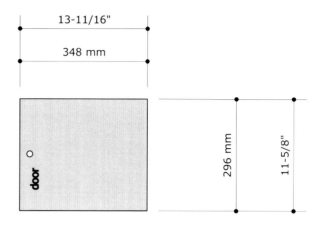

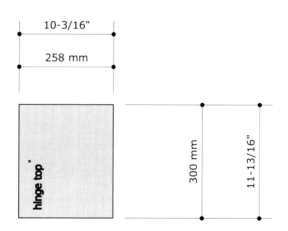

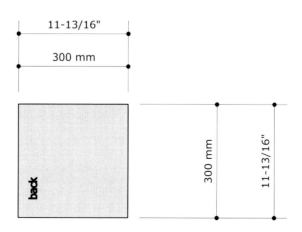

Making It

The following illustrations show how to make the trap.

Before starting, read and familiarise yourself with these instructions.

Drill pilot holes before inserting the screws.

Place the bottom on the work surface.

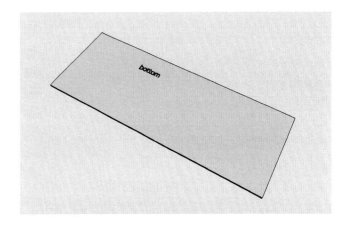

Fix the battens.
The battens at the front should be set back enough to allow room for the trapdoor and its side battens. To be sure, set them back an extra 3/4" (19mm).

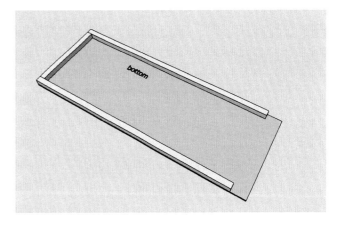

Fix the back panel to the bottom.

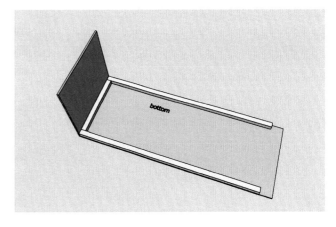

Then fix battens to the back panel.

Note how the top batten is set 1/4" (6mm) down from the top (this being the thickness of the plywood).

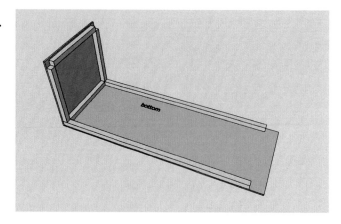

Fix one of the side panels.

Drill some ventilation holes in the side panel.

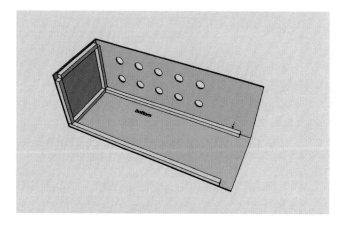

Then fix the top batten, once again positioned 1/4" (6mm) down from the top, so it lines up with the top batten on the rear panel.

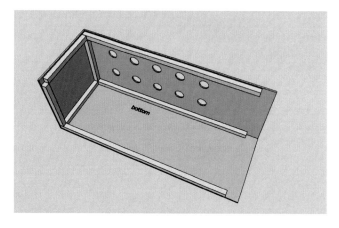

Then fix the other side panel.

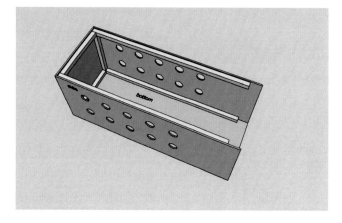

Now fix the trapdoor guide battens.

They should be about 2' (600mm) long.

Make sure that the gap between them is slightly greater - about 1/8" (2mm) than the thickness of the trapdoor, so that it can slide easily.

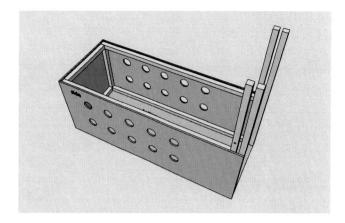

Put the trap door in position. You'll need to cut, plane or sand off a little from the sides so that there's no rubbing against the side panels.

Add two short battens at the top as extra support.

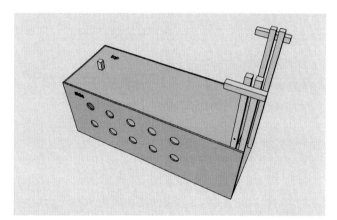

Before fitting the lid, cut a hole for the prop. This can be a small rectangle, or a circular hole. It needs to be slightly larger than the prop.

And cut notches at the front to fit around the battens.

If you're using the trap to catch larger animals, like cats, just make the lid about 3/4" (19mm) shorter and leave a gap between it and the trapdoor guide battens.

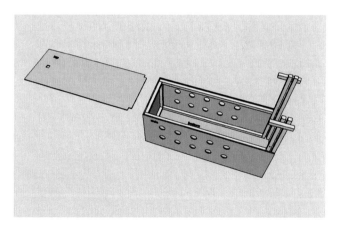

Then temporarily put the prop in position. It should project above the lid by about 1 1/2" (40mm).

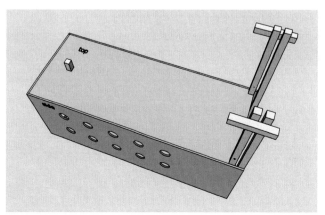

Now make the pivot mechanism.

Cut the notches at the front large enough to allow a small gap between the hinge bottom and the trapdoor guide battens.

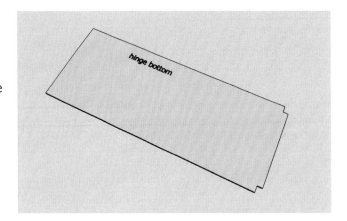

Then the hinge top panel.

Note that it's set forward of the notches.

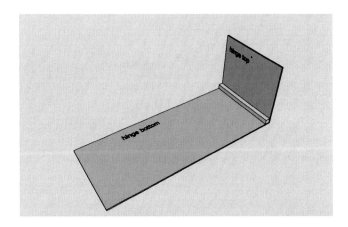

Then screw a corner batten and the side stiffening battens in place.

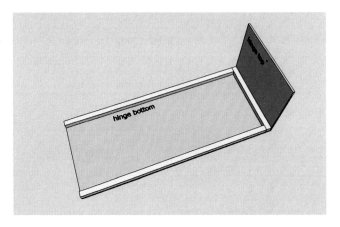

The counterweight goes here.

I've shown an empty cat food tin, screwed in place.

Put stones in the tin as required to overcome any friction.

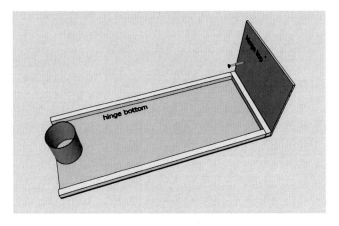

This is how the pivot mechanism is hinged.

Drill a hole on the trapdoor support batten, about 1 1/2" (40mm) above the lid. The hole should be larger than the screw to allow it to pivot.

Put the screw through the batten and into the pivot mechanism.

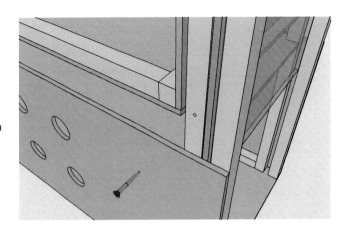

The engineers amongst you will point out that there will be frictional losses and a tendency for the hinge to slide. So - as an alternative, you could use steel nails or metal bar, fitted into a tight hole in the pivot mechanism and a loose hole in the trapdoor support batten.

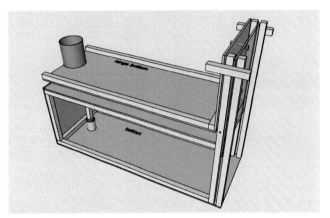

Then set the trap so that the prop rests on some food in the food tube.

Then place a screw in a tight hole in the hinge top. Set the screw so that it just holds the trapdoor open, and a very small downward movement of the prop will release it. You'll probably need to adjust the length of the prop by cutting it shorter.

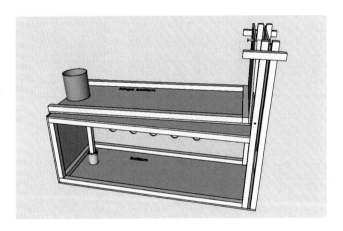

That's it!

Experiment with different types of food and food tray. The prop can easily be cut shorter - or cut a new piece of wood to the required length.

Also experiment with the weight of the counterweight by putting more, or less stones in the empty tin.

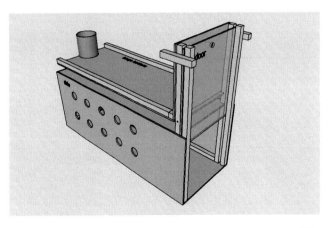

Just scale the drawings down to make a smaller (mouse) trap, or up to make a bigger (dog) trap.

Happy hunting!

CPSIA information can be obtained
at www.ICGtesting.com
Printed in the USA
LVXC02n0219121213
364982LV00012B/47